Transcendental Studies

Transcendental Studies

graphics of poetic intent

being one possible play
in the Glass Bead Game

by Keith Wilson

new west classics 4

chax press   tucson   2003

Acknowledgments

Some of the poems in this book have been printed in the
following magazines:
> *Sin Fronteras Journal*
> *Etudes*, Limberlost Press
> "Still Life" appears in *Bosque Redondo*, Penny
> Whistle Press, but was first in this book.

ISBN 0-925904-38-4

Library of Congress Cataloging-in-Publication Data

Wilson, Keith, 1927-
   Transcendental studies : graphics of poetic intent :
being one possible play in the glass bead game / by Keith
Wilson.
      p. cm. — (New West classics ; 4)
   ISBN 0-925904-38-4 (pbk. : alk. paper)
   I. Title. II. Series.
   PS3573.I457T73 2003
   811'.54—dc21

                    2003006741

to Roge Besmilr Brigham

to Robert Duncan
who showed me the way

Contents

"An intimate book in the hands and in the mind."

— Charles Alexander

Compound all the Seasons

into a vision
                    forms

themselves magic

as glass

                    a window

in a Llano icestorm

all crystal

all light

eyes for a wolf's howl

in form the wind

vortexes of the land

's   own song

                              —for Stanley Noyes

The Fabled Fool

And the gold-edged chasm
is a step beneath his
flowered foot

        the bright
the air   the rock
hewn smile of centuries

a cry

        hung

on an Easterning wind —

       and a fall

       that seems more

        a rising

The Motorcycle Rider

—for Drummond Hadley

Doppler's effect, the stuttering here at
the edge of hearing, growing to roar, chromed
mufflers in the sun—the man sitting small amidst
auras of light, noise: straight-backed, slim
he comes, riding the air as if it were the motor—
his laugh rips off into the wind, his
sound, a great sweep across emptying place.

WHO

ever

THOUGHT

we

WERE

RATIONAL?

[moon
　　[clouds
　　　　[stars

　　　　　　　[blackness

eden
apples

probably
didn't

taste
any

sweeter
than blue

your lips
in near

darkness
rustling

in
the   sheets
first   drifting
place

moon

?   clouds

— for Larry and Lenore

IT IS

night

Hawk

blood

on spurs of grass

—IT IS

the drying

eyes

as the moon rises

&

Cabal

The wind

        conspires against

        that tree.

Look,

it has already

           blown the moon/[sun]
           into its branches

and set all the leaves
afire.

        — for Nancy Noyes

The Red Balloon

string
  trailing
       d
          o
            w
               n
all the blue
heavens
    gather
          -ing

           to

          BURST!

     it, still
     it slips
     nudging its
     way through

       the air

         up
         &
         up
         &
         up
         &

              — to Janey Slagle
                on her birthday
                  it arrives

Marriage Poem

I am
the wind she
said you
know me you
have always
known
me

— for Robin & Nancy Hastings
  on the occasion of their marriage

Blue/Stone

where lights of sky
touch grey, they meld
it to form strata
above the desert

sands and under them
the rock holds at its center
silence: the unflawed blue
the stone

— for Robert & Jean Davis

Etude

Now

       the dawn

                                (horizon
                  breaks   pink
                              flaming
                                        red)
      night's hold

        and throws

          light

(confetti)

                  all over

                           my mountains

       and me

        — for Charles and Danny

Diptych

The Poet	The Poet's Wife
stands	looks strangely
beside	like him, his strain
himself	too often on her face
with	her eye turns when
words	he speaks, but away
in	there have simply been
his	too many words how
hands	ever beautiful to
are	one not used to the
empty	
	power of flayed expression
	and she numb to them, him
are	she is lovely, he
dreams	knows it but stands
in his	silent, words exhausted
eyes	

— from two prints by Paul Klee
and for Theodore Enslin

The Pubic Self

before a mirror

and how I appear

    sexually

at 64

with little

to show

much to conceal

        — for me, of course

        (with apologies
         to WCW

Graphology

I write, he writes, she writes

/marks on paper/scratches on walls/

A

D
R
A
W
I
N
G

moose or bear

maybe a rabbit?

my girl's face

with two hearts

I put cries on pages
he said I grow tired
of words and I hear
crying everywhere
I go

below?

— for Uncle Gene

22

We know in part
prophesy in part
The rest we make up.

—Robert Kabac

what is this poem
that I have spent
my life all of it
pursuing?

Paintings aren't color
they're geometry and
eye cones, light
have little to do with
canvas, wood, glass

the smile
of any one of my
daughters the look
in my son's eyes

hobo art, scratches
on the gates of heaven

all are of more
value and yet
   the

   poem

opened me, closed
me around them I believe
angels did walk
with Blake and he
saw Them through
his poem, the
poem, you see?

— for Bob

23

Indiana Odyssey

Here again the rich green
land heavy air almost drowns
the days, holds all in such
mists

                heat
bears down straight like the pressure
of a palm might do, corn ripples
as we pass stray winds catch tassels
rattle of thunder
              ahead

              the Continent

              opening before us

              — for Kathy and Walt

White Blossoms

pressed under stone
blow fragile
in a later wind

between my
fingertips
—these gentle locusts

— for April

Mountain Still Life

mauve.

tree rustle

& a sort of green

light blue

maybe some

stark
grey

clouds!

darklined

to frame the desert
horizon and the

light

— for Everett Campbell

The Sterling Boston Co. Ladies' Pen (1913)

each time,
this pen
writes
perfectly

a hummingbird
thrusting its gold
into the opening flower
of this untouched page

— for Peter Wichert

Now

is when the sun
runs the sky

and a warm wind
hides the mountain

in light dust
                    arroyos

flow gold through shadows
too heavy with history

                    spirit songs
ghost drums

                    & the thunder
ing buffalo darken the sage

Old Mountains Old Mountains
watching, watching always always
Old Mountains Old Mountains

                    — for Harold Littlebird
                       & his songs

28

Granddaughter,

To me, you will always
be Changing Woman, Lady
of Light even though I
know you are too tiny
now for these great names
to seem the same as you
sleeping in my hands
(which band us as one)
but the day will come
when the world succumbs
to what I see trace it
self on your face.

— for Diana Marie Oyemna Fox

klangfarbenmelodie

ROSES

don't grow
well
in this
sand wind
whips
even
the thorns
away

— for Caitlin

the sun

slips through these red hills

darkness

blossoms into a fresh clear

day

of birdsongs and thin clouds

Canyonland
Arizona
Late Summer

— for George Vlahos
Watercolorist

Overheard Conversation

"She says, he says, behind
them both canyons and mesas
of winds that speak into their ears—
What chance have either of them,
she, hearing her mother, he,
trying to avoid imitating the father
he abhors. The wind, how easy
it is to blame it all on the wind,
or the dryness of desert days
they, caught into a web of years
full of suffering, the battle
of men and women fighting in animal
masks, pipes shrilling about them, knowing
nothing they do or say. The night
it rushes to surround them."

— for Eric

The First Morning

What kind

of

a dawn

might

that

have been

— a slow, easy

flowering

of light

against an

unprepared

sky

— for Heloise
who admired it

All the seeds
where
            they are found
capture the sun
                earth

hold them

                gold.
            brown.

            release them!

                BLOOMS

                DARKNESS

34

Fossil

locked
within
this beauty
this stone river
flowing into
my hand

this bird's
lost breath

— for Jeremiah

SkyScape

one

     sun

      one

        moon

    in
     a
      thrice

       stars!

        &

     dex

       ter

         ous

        comets

      playing

        at being

       clowns

        — for Klee

the night

it passes
like some sort
of train
we never quite
    caught

and sunrise?

it forever
delivers us up
   unaware

   unprepared

Sudden Storm

leaves

    swirl

        goldedges

    quick

        slashes

            of light

          from the center

          of thunder

          a following

          silence

       — for Ewa Blass

Doric

Winds cut stone
leave channels
to enter crystal
Greek nightworlds

lost granite boys
marbled girls

— for Kristin Mavournin

Moontide

And the ship
hulled down

yard lights
glimmering

slips outward
with only

the creaking
of blocks

as sails rise,
swell in the land breeze

moon strikes a golden path
across a black sea.

— for Janet & Nathaniel

Funerary Object

My uncle, did I kill him by missing
his funeral? The world spins under
my fingers and the wind blows caskets
across the sky, choruses of angels
sing from every pin and I, chanting, become
one with the sweeping wind, the sustaining
capstoned bluffs so stark against this
falling snow

— for Keith Wyman Edwards

The Sign

a moccasin
print
in damp
      sand
   gnats
   buzzing about

one half
  -eaten

        l
          e
            a
              f

the scent

  you

  left

   in

  this

  room

                — for Helowiggles

flowers

fall

petal

by

petal

into

the quiet pool

before

me

darkening

— for Jill Somoza

Abstraction

whirling
the leaves
the autumn
get lost

in oranged
obscurities
skirls

of   wind

&
the
catspaw

scent
of
you

Afternoon

lizard

    tongue

flicks

    in/out!

sheen

  on

    fly's
      wing hot

  silent sun

Spring Canyon

—Florida Mountains, New Mexico

It happened where
when I was a little boy
I traced with my finger
the strange marks recording
Apache visits, hunting notes

I called the place "Apache Spring."
It was near there, Gary fell

                            falling

did he fall straight

                        or

                        t
                        u
                          m
                          b
                            l
                            e

was he killed
instantly?

or lingered
the light
held in his eyes
for at least
a moment
or two

a crescendo
of sounds

fading?

— for Gary Garwood
a good man, with a good heart
who loved mountains
October 4, 1991

Three Minutes After Twelve

one note
        leaning toward
dawn
        and whatever stands
behind that note
                old Leadbelly
mourning on a barely born Christmas day
the old dead voice
singing out from everything
that bound him and you
and me and all of us
                    a sound like the tearing of skin
                    or a distant flaming tree
                     or Christ dying

                                his cross against
                                a mottled sky

            that morning, this sun
            the same that saw
            Him born, saw Him
            die
                a second later
                        nails
                wood
                        blood

            dripping to sand

the horizons
are on fire.
gunfire.

too far
to hear
the screams
or smell
the blood
the ruptured
intestines

— for Victor diSuvero

Now is

        — whatever

we receive it

as

       a moonflower

         sacred datura

          o, opening

             closing

      the horizontal sky
      aflame with new day

the light

really

    never

        fails

           it
          is
            only

          our

            eyes

— for Roxanne

Evensong

It is evening again.
My son and his son
sit on the patio, a breeze
catches my grandson's blonde hair,
his father's darkly intense face
leans over his seven-year-old tranquility.

I, a shadow, soon to vanish
watch, hear their voices
as water flowing over
mountain stones or light
caught just before dusk
by surprise, all is held
here in the closing darkness.

— for Kevin & Jeremiah
with much love
September 16, 1991

52

Still Life

too bright, too
bright the
sun on falling

feathers, the hawk
redbreasted, bullet
smashed

there leaps one
flicker of life
eye turning fierce

before the beak
clatters
drops

its pale tongue
streaked by the light
of early morning

— Cambray, New Mexico
for my father and mother

Blue

mountain stones
in light
creek
bottom

lapis streaks
through
flowing
diamond

— for Bill and Pat Miles

the darkness.

How
it crowds

just beyond

my fingers

as they write

these words

— for Kevin

The Lake at Full Night

mosquitos
have always
loved me

but even they
cannot spoil
this evening

when silence
fills the
water before me

— for Jennifer

Desert Still Life

The whitethorn mesquite
bloomed today, tiny yellow
puffballs on the delicate
branches of Spring, a clear
wind blowing from the Organ
Mountains, tranquil and blue
with a dark suggestion of rain
clouds about their sharp crests

—the sense of flower, the honeyed air.

— for Alexandra Eggena

Now is

    —whatever

  we receive it

as

        a moonflower

        sacred datura

        opening

        door

        closing

  the horizontal sky
  aflame with new day

always
I
remember
yours
face
the
sweet
light
surrounding

it

— for M.V.E.

The Snow

comes like a stranger
here where wind
is the music dust
the rain

Now heavy
flakes fall on cactus
I would swear are surprised
caught naked

before the stunning
cold—a kind of white
darkness moistly

closing our eyes
as we walk toward
the rough outline
of our house

> December 24, 1990
> Organ Mountains
> Las Cruces, New Mexico

— for Kerrin
whose birthday it is

Etude

for

ever

is

too long

for

this

butterfly

morning

in spring

— for Frodo

The Following Sea

                              full and bye

  it dogs me, the waves, smell of
  kelp and rotting islands

                                   the coves
   and lagoons in summer's
   moon light gleaming
across waters I once knew, behind
the me I once knew
that following sea....

New West Classics

Book 1: Nathaniel Tarn, *The Architextures*
Book 2: David Bromige, *As in T as in Tether*
Book 3: Beverly Dahlen, *A-Reading Spicer and*
            Eighteen Sonnets (forthcoming)
Book 4: Keith Wilson, *Transcendental Studies*

The New West Classics series publishes essential new
works by established writers from the Rocky Mountain
States to the West Coast of North America; particularly
writers whose innovative and/or experimental directions
generally set them outside ordinary considerations of
what constitutes "western" literature in America. Chax
Press believes that the practice of the most innovative,
visionary, and experimental writers of the west must be
included in future definitions of western writing.